Thinking Critically:
School Shootings
and Violence

Other titles in the *Thinking Critically* series include:

Thinking Critically:
School Shootings
and Violence

John Allen

ReferencePoint
Press®

San Diego, CA

© 2020 ReferencePoint Press, Inc.
Printed in the United States

For more information, contact:
ReferencePoint Press, Inc.
PO Box 27779
San Diego, CA 92198
www.ReferencePointPress.com

Picture Credits:
cover: Hayk_Shalunts/Shutterstock.com
10: fitzcrittle/Shutterstock.com
Charts and graphs by Maury Aaseng

LIBRARY OF CONGRESS CATALOGING-IN-PUBLICATION DATA

Names: Allen, John, 1957– author.
Title: Thinking Critically: School Shootings and Violence/by John Allen.
Other titles: Thinking Critically: School Shootings and Violence
Description: San Diego, CA: ReferencePoint Press, Inc., [2019] | Series: Thinking Critically |
    Audience: Grade 9 to 12. | Includes bibliographical references and index.
Identifiers: LCCN 2019007511 (print) | LCCN 2019011039 (ebook) | ISBN 9781682826645 (eBook)
    | ISBN 9781682826638 (hardback)
Subjects: LCSH: School shootings—United States—Prevention—Juvenile literature. | School
    violence—United States—Prevention—Juvenile literature.
Classification: LCC LB3013.32 (ebook) | LCC LB3013.32 .A55 2019 (print) | DDC 371.7/82—dc23
LC record available at https://lccn.loc.gov/2019007511

Contents

Foreword

"Literacy is the most basic currency of the knowledge economy we're living in today." Barack Obama (at the time a senator from Illinois) spoke these words during a 2005 speech before the American Library Association. One question raised by this statement is: What does it mean to be a literate person in the twenty-first century?

E.D. Hirsch Jr., author of *Cultural Literacy: What Every American Needs to Know*, answers the question this way: "To be culturally literate is to possess the basic information needed to thrive in the modern world. The breadth of the information is great, extending over the major domains of human activity from sports to science."

But literacy in the twenty-first century goes beyond the accumulation of knowledge gained through study and experience and expanded over time. Now more than ever literacy requires the ability to sift through and evaluate vast amounts of information and, as the authors of the Common Core State Standards state, to "demonstrate the cogent reasoning and use of evidence that is essential to both private deliberation and responsible citizenship in a democratic republic."

The *Thinking Critically* series challenges students to become discerning readers, to think independently, and to engage and develop their skills as critical thinkers. Through a narrative-driven, pro/con format, the series introduces students to the complex issues that dominate public discourse—topics such as gun control and violence, social networking, and medical marijuana. Each chapter revolves around a single, pointed question such as Can Stronger Gun Control Measures Prevent Mass Shootings?, or Does Social Networking Benefit Society?, or Should Medical Marijuana Be Legalized? This inquiry-based approach introduces student researchers to core issues and concerns on a given topic. Each chapter includes one part that argues the affirmative and one part that argues the negative—all written by a single author. With the single-author format the predominant arguments for and against an issue can be synthesized into clear, accessible discussions supported by details and evidence including relevant facts, direct quotes, current examples, and statistical illustrations. All volumes include focus questions to guide students as they read each pro/con discussion, a list of key facts, and an annotated list of related organizations and websites for conducting further research.

The authors of the Common Core State Standards have set out the particular qualities that a literate person in the twenty-first century must have. These include the ability to think independently, establish a base of knowledge across a wide range of subjects, engage in open-minded but discerning reading and listening, know how to use and evaluate evidence, and appreciate and understand diverse perspectives. The new *Thinking Critically* series supports these goals by providing a solid introduction to the study of pro/con issues.

School Shootings and Violence

Superintendent Trent Lovett had to fight back tears as he recalled the day it happened. On the morning of January 23, 2018, a fifteen-year-old student named Gabe Parker had carried his stepfather's 9-millimeter handgun into the common area at Marshall County High School in eastern Kentucky. Parker began spraying bullets into a crowd of milling students, then dropped the gun and faded into the chaotic scene. Amid screams and sobs, teachers tried to herd the students into safe rooms. Police and medics arrived to find young people lying in pools of blood. In all, sixteen students were shot, and two died from their wounds. Months afterward, Lovett spoke to the county's School Safety Working Group. Seated next to him were the parents of Bailey Holt and Preston Cope, the two slain students. Lovett talked about ways to prevent such a nightmare from happening again. He talked about mental health counseling, and others on the committee brought up metal detectors. But Lovett kept returning to the parents. "My seat here is much easier than theirs," said Lovett. "January 23 was a trying day for all of us. One of our students took out two of his classmates and injured several others. I never thought I'd see the things I saw that day."[1]

Growing Fears

The horror of school shootings has become all too familiar to Americans in recent years. Names of schools and towns where some of the worst incidents have taken place live on in public memory: Columbine,

Virginia Tech, Sandy Hook, Umpqua, Parkland. Like Trent Lovett, education officials around the country agonize over ways to prevent gun violence in schools. Commissions are formed to study the problem, and experts from law enforcement and building security to mental health weigh in with their professional advice. Following the shootings that left seventeen dead and fourteen wounded at Marjory Stoneman Douglas (MSD) High School in Parkland, Florida, on February 14, 2018, President Donald Trump declared, "No child, teacher or anyone else should ever feel unsafe in an American school."[2] Yet for some the fear of gun violence persists on a daily basis. Lisette Rozenblet says her daughter, who was at the high school in Parkland, had bad feelings about the possibility of such an incident. "Her biggest fear is a school shooting," says Rozenblet. "She is always begging me to be home-schooled because she was scared of this."[3]

The problem of school shootings appears to be growing. According to the journal *Education Week*, 2018 was the worst year yet for gun attacks in American schools. In a yearlong tracking project, *Education Week* recorded 23 incidents of gun violence in schools, with 113 people killed or injured. Victims included the 17 killed at MSD High School and another 10 slain at Santa Fe High School near Houston, Texas, on May 18, 2018. With most districts having 180 school days in a year, shootings occurred on average once every 8 school days. The *Washington Post* noted that the number of schoolchildren who lost their lives in school shootings in 2018 was nearly twice the number of military service personnel killed overseas the same year.

> "Her biggest fear is a school shooting. She is always begging me to be home-schooled because she was scared of this."[3]
>
> —Lisette Rozenblet, whose daughter attends the high school in Parkland, Florida, where a school shooting took place

Gun violence in schools is part of a disturbing trend toward mass shootings in American society overall. School shootings elicit special outrage due to the youth and innocence of most of the victims. Yet many worry that little is being done to reverse the trend. In 1999 the nation was shocked by the shooting deaths of thirteen people at Columbine High School in Littleton, Colorado—at the time, the worst high school gun massacre in US history. Since Columbine, 223 more victims have lost their lives in school shootings. In fact, the Columbine tragedy no longer ranks in the top ten of deadliest mass shootings nationwide.

Despite their huge emotional impact, school shootings remain statistically very rare. Crime experts point out that school shootings with multiple victims occur on average about once per year, in a nation with more than one hundred thousand schools. James Alan Fox, a professor of criminology at Northeastern University in Boston, Massachusetts, says the problem was worse in the 1990s. In the 1997–1998 school year, for example, there were four multiple-victim school shootings in the United States. Fox found that 0.55 students per million were shot and killed in the 1992–1993 school year, compared to 0.15 per million in 2014–2015. He believes American schools are actually safer today than in previous decades.

In the wake of the deadly shooting at Marjory Stoneman Douglas High School in Florida, students, parents, teachers, and other supporters march to demand that legislators pass stronger gun laws.

Garen Wintemute, an emergency room physician at the University of California–Davis Medical Center, has researched school gun violence and agrees with Fox's viewpoint. "Schools are just about the safest place in the world for kids to be," says Wintemute. "Although each [shooting] is horrific and rivets the entire nation for a period of time, mass shootings at schools are really very uncommon, and they are not increasing in frequency. What's changed is how aware we are of them."[4]

Profiles of School Shooters

Due to intense media coverage, the public has become aware of the general profile of school shooters. Time and again the perpetrator is revealed to be a troubled male teenager with access to firearms. School shooters tend to have issues with depression and rage toward others. They plan their attacks carefully and often leave behind clues to their intentions. They see themselves as outcasts and usually find it difficult to maintain friendships. Committing mass murder may be attractive to them as a way to become famous. Frequent thoughts about violence and suicide can make them into silent powder kegs on the brink of exploding.

For example, the two gunmen who killed twelve fellow students and a teacher at Columbine in 1999 recorded their violent thoughts before carrying out the massacre. Dylan Klebold and Eric Harris discussed their plot in journal entries and secretly recorded videos. From this evidence FBI profilers and psychologists determined that Klebold seemed to have severe depression and suicidal thoughts. Harris showed signs of being a psychopath—a person with violent social behavior—who fantasized about getting revenge on his enemies. Klebold and Harris committed suicide by gunshot in the library where they had killed ten of their victims.

> "Although each [shooting] is horrific and rivets the entire nation for a period of time, mass shootings at schools are really very uncommon, and they are not increasing in frequency. What's changed is how aware we are of them."[4]
>
> —Garen Wintemute, an emergency room physician at the University of California–Davis Medical Center

News reports also revealed facts about Nikolas Cruz, the shooter in Parkland, Florida. As a boy, Cruz delighted in torturing small animals. Classmates said he was a loner who would stare moodily at people he encountered. Foul language and disruptive behavior made him a constant problem in the classroom. In January 2017 Cruz was expelled from MSD High School for assaulting another student. He also dropped out of his mental health treatments. A month after being kicked out of school, Cruz purchased the AR-15 rifle he would use in the massacre. The day of the shooting, he posted a chilling video on Facebook in which he announced his intention to kill at least twenty people and make himself famous. There could hardly have been more red flags about an individual—police were contacted about Cruz nearly forty times over the years. Nonetheless, Cruz, like other troubled teenage shooters, had slipped through the cracks.

Calls for Gun Control

School shootings inevitably bring calls for stronger gun laws. After Parkland, for example, gun control advocates expressed outrage at how easily Cruz, with his history of mental problems and bad behavior, had been able to obtain an assault rifle. A number of Parkland students began to speak out against assault weapons and what they considered to be lax gun laws. Led by fellow student David Hogg, these young people organized the Never Again movement to press for stricter background checks for gun buyers. They also set up the March for Our Lives, a student-led protest on March 24, 2018, that attracted more than 1 million supporters in Washington, DC, and many other cities. The status of the Parkland students as survivors of a horrific school attack gave their movement added credibility that went beyond normal politics.

Supporters of gun rights have weighed in as well. Many insisted the problem was not with a legally purchased weapon but with mental health policies that failed to protect the public from a young person with such obvious violent tendencies. Some suggested that teachers and school officials should be armed themselves to deal with emergencies on school property. As in the aftermath of other mass shootings, public opinion was split into the usual pro- and anti-gun-control positions.

Searching for Answers

Like those at Marshall County High School in Kentucky, school officials, parents, and students around the country continue to search for ways to prevent school shootings. Some schools have started outreach programs to help identify potentially dangerous students. Students are urged to report early signs of trouble such as violent social media posts and threatening remarks. Some have suggested that social media companies become more active in reporting online threats to authorities. Parents are prompted to check on their children's social media use and keep an eye on their relationships and any unusual behavior. Some believe better security systems and armed guards are the key to preventing school shootings. "I wish we could guarantee something like that will never happen again but I can't do it," says Trent Lovett. "We want these students to feel safe and we are doing everything we can to ensure that."[5]

Chapter One

Should Schools Be Equipped with Metal Detectors?

Schools Should Be Equipped with Metal Detectors

- Metal detectors enable schools to discover and confiscate weapons from anyone entering the school building or campus.
- The presence of a metal detector helps prevent violence by convincing potential attackers they will likely be caught if they try to smuggle in a weapon.
- Metal detectors promote peace of mind among students, staff, and parents that a school has a safe atmosphere.

The Debate at a Glance

Schools Should Not Be Equipped with Metal Detectors

- The cost of installing metal detectors in schools is too high to be practical.
- By creating a false sense of security, metal detectors can divert staff from practical ways of preventing violence.
- Use of metal detectors can stigmatize schools that are poor, urban, or minority based.

Schools Should Be Equipped with Metal Detectors

"I walk through the metal detectors daily. Guards check my bag, and on days of heightened security, I may have to show ID. I don't question it; I find solace in knowing the origins, in knowing that I'll be safe while I work."

—Joy Mohammed, a teacher at an inner-city Detroit high school

Joy Mohammed, "Opinion: In Defense of School Metal Detectors," School Leaders Now, April 11, 2018. https://schoolleadersnow.weareteachers.com.

Consider these questions as you read:

1. Do you agree that installing metal detectors in schools makes schools safer? Why or why not?
2. Do you believe that using metal detectors to screen everyone who enters a school building is practical? Explain your answer.
3. When considering the value of metal detectors in schools, should the importance of peace of mind outweigh concerns about cost? Explain your answer.

Editor's note: The discussion that follows presents common arguments made in support of this perspective, reinforced by facts, quotes, and examples taken from various sources.

Metal detectors are a vital element in preventing school shootings. In order to keep firearms and other weapons out of schools, it is necessary first to detect them in the possession of those trying to enter the school. Once found, a gun can be confiscated and the offender dealt with by school authorities or the police. There is no simpler, more cost-effective way to prevent students or other persons from sneaking firearms into a school building. "Would it work? Just ask Congress," writes parent Rebecca Wendlandt to the *Spokesman-Review* in Spokane, Washington. "You can't get into the Capitol without going through [a metal detector]. . . . Since the U.S. can afford metal detectors and armed guards for [Congress], are they more important than our children?"[6]

There are many good reasons to install metal detectors in schools. They are reliable, having been employed successfully at airports, arenas, office buildings, and other public facilities for years. Simply the presence of a metal detector can dissuade a potential shooter from even trying to smuggle in a firearm. The use of metal detectors also promotes peace of mind for students, parents, teachers, and school officials.

An Effective Safety Measure

Installing a metal detector at a school entryway is one of the most effective safety measures available. A metal detector can be in the form of a walk-through unit or a wand (handheld scanner) wielded by a security guard. Either type can detect guns, knives, or other prohibited objects hidden in an individual's clothes or in a bag, purse, or backpack. Proper use of a metal detector makes it very difficult for a potential school shooter to smuggle a firearm into a school building.

School districts that have invested in metal detectors have seen incidents involving weapons decline significantly. For example, the Aldine Independent School District in Houston, Texas, is one of two districts in the area that have installed metal detectors in all its schools. Aldine schools have seen the number of weapons incidents each school year fall from an average of 12 to 2.3. Houston's Spring Independent School District has seen a similar decline. After the Santa Fe High School shooting in May 2018, other schools in the area and around the nation have looked into installing their own metal detectors.

Some critics argue that metal detectors in schools are not practical, because it takes too long to check everyone entering the school each morning. However, students at Aldine schools accept the practice as part of their morning routine. Most students arrive at school a bit earlier than before. They line up in an orderly way, take off their coats and jackets, set aside their cell phones or laptops, and hand over their backpacks and bags to be examined. The whole process takes only a few minutes. It is much like entering an airport preflight or a sports arena before a game. At any rate, US representative Kay Granger of Texas, a former teacher, thinks worries about time and logistics are overblown. "Some people say there will be lines, they'll have to stand outside forever," says Granger. "I said they don't do that at the airports. When they put metal detectors at the airports, the planes took off at the same time. People got there earlier. They planned that."[7]

A Deterrent That Works

Just the presence of metal detectors at school entryways tells potential shooters they will be caught if they try to smuggle in a firearm. As a result, few will even try, making metal detectors a deterrent that works. As long as metal detectors are kept in place and operated properly, the problem of gun violence inside schools will be greatly reduced. "These machines are definitely a deterrent," says Joe Vazquez, director of security sales for Garrett Metal Detectors. "Someone who has at least some hesitancy with what they're doing will probably reconsider if they see a checkpoint with a metal detector."[8]

To find proof of how metal detectors deter shootings, one need look no further than urban schools in large cities like New York, Chicago, Detroit, and Los Angeles. Security experts note that many urban schools have been employing metal detectors since the 1980s with great success. For example, the New York Police Department reports that 2,120 weapons were confiscated in New York City high schools in the 2016–2017 school year. About half were discovered due to metal detectors. Almost all mass shootings in America have taken place in suburban or rural schools, where metal detectors are

> "These machines are definitely a deterrent. Someone who has at least some hesitancy with what they're doing will probably reconsider if they see a checkpoint with a metal detector."[8]
>
> —Joe Vazquez, director of security sales for Garrett Metal Detectors

much less prevalent. For example, at MSD High School in Parkland, Florida, Nikolas Cruz had no trouble entering the school building with a duffel bag containing an AR-15 rifle. Faced with a metal detector like the ones found in large urban schools, Cruz likely would not even have made the attempt. "I think urban schools are eons ahead," says Philip Smith, president of the National African American Gun Association. "They've been dealing with violence a lot longer than suburban schools."[9]

The Value of Peace of Mind

Another advantage of metal detectors is the peace of mind they offer. With these devices monitoring school doors, students and their parents can feel confident that firearms or other weapons will not find their way inside. No security method is foolproof. But metal detectors, with their strong track record of preventing gun violence at schools and other venues, have earned the confidence of ordinary citizens.

Peace of mind plays a crucial role in their use. For example, heightened anxiety about recent gun attacks led the Bayonne School District in New Jersey to expand its use of metal detectors. Bayonne installed its first metal detector at the local high school in 1996. After the shooting in Parkland, Florida, Superintendent Michael Wanko and the Bayonne school board sought to ease fears going forward. According to Wanko, "The board decided it would be in the best interest to make everyone feel more comfortable to have metal detectors in each of our schools."[10] Soon grade schools and middle schools in Bayonne will all be equipped with the walk-through devices. School boards around the country would be wise to follow Bayonne's lead on this issue.

> "The board decided it would be in the best interest to make everyone feel more comfortable to have metal detectors in each of our schools."[10]
>
> —Superintendent Michael Wanko of the Bayonne School District in Bayonne, New Jersey

Those who question the cost of placing metal detectors in school entryways are ignoring the even greater value of peace of mind. Representative Granger is one of several lawmakers offering federal plans to pay for

Metal Detectors Can Lower the Number of Weapons Incidents in Schools

The Aldine Independent School District in Houston, Texas, equipped its schools with more than two hundred metal detectors around the 2009–2010 school year. Since then, the number of weapons incidents has dropped by nearly ten per year—a clear example of the benefits of metal detectors in schools.

Weapons Incidents at Aldine Independent School District

metal detectors in schools. Granger's proposal would make $500 million in federal grant money available over the next ten years to help schools pay for metal detectors. To be eligible for the funds, schools would have to submit detailed safety plans for placement of metal detectors. Fort Worth police chief Joel Fitzgerald has discussed the proposal with Granger and considers it promising. "Any proposal seeking to reinforce the sense of safety and security for our students is a welcome change to the status quo,"[11] says Fitzgerald. Like parents and school officials, he knows that students need to feel safe and secure at school in order to succeed.

Installing metal detectors at school entryways is an excellent way to prevent guns and other weapons from being smuggled into schools. These devices have been used for decades and are known to be effective and practical. Simply the presence of a metal detector can convince a potential shooter that it is useless to try to sneak a firearm into the building. In addition, metal detectors provide peace of mind for students and their parents. By helping create a safe atmosphere at school, they ease fears about violence. Rather than worrying about cost, school boards should work with the federal government to find ways to pay for more metal detectors in schools.

Schools Should Not Be Equipped with Metal Detectors

"Even a well-run school metal detector program is not 100% foolproof. Any security technology is only as effective as the human element behind the equipment."

—Ken Trump, president of National School Safety and Security Services

Ken Trump, "School Metal Detectors," National School Safety and Security Services. www.schoolsecurity.org.

Consider these questions as you read:

1. Judging by the facts and ideas presented in this discussion, how persuasive is the argument that installing metal detectors in school is too expensive? Explain your answer.
2. Do you agree that use of metal detectors in schools can provide school officials with a false sense of security and actually make students less safe? Why or why not?
3. What do you think it means to say that metal detectors stigmatize minority or urban schools? Do you agree that this is true? Explain.

Editor's note: The discussion that follows presents common arguments made in support of this perspective, reinforced by facts, quotes, and examples taken from various sources.

Installing metal detectors in schools is far from the best solution for preventing school shootings. It is tempting to think that these devices can keep guns and other weapons from being smuggled into school buildings. However, metal detectors have many drawbacks. They are very expensive to purchase, maintain, and operate properly. Since their effectiveness is so overhyped, they can lead school staff to neglect more practical ways of checking on students and spotting possible trouble areas. In addition, metal detectors can create a depressing prison-like atmosphere in schools. They tend to stigmatize urban or minority-based schools as being prone to violence.

Not Worth the High Cost

Security experts agree that metal detectors generally are not worth their high price tag. Models suitable for schools tend to cost from $4,000 to $5,000. Boston officials claim to have paid about $4,800 apiece for the city's walk-through metal detectors, plus $140 apiece for handheld wands. Michael White, eastern region director for Security Detection, notes that large schools generally require four or five units to run students through the system each morning. White estimates the cost for installing metal detector systems at the five high schools in Worcester, Massachusetts, at $73,000 to $91,250. Cities must have a large tax base to support such spending.

Those who clamor for metal detectors in every public school tend to ignore the massive cost. In response to such calls, South Carolina's Revenue and Fiscal Affairs Office found that outfitting every public school in the state with metal detectors would have an initial cost of $14.4 million. And that does not include the annual $98.3 million necessary to train staff members and post them at security checkpoints. Metal detectors do not operate by themselves. Although they give off an alarm signal if tripped, trained personnel still must check the source of the alarm and decide how to handle the situation.

Moreover, simply installing metal detectors does not necessarily prevent guns, knives, and other weapons from getting into school buildings. Ken Trump, president of National School Safety and Security Services, points out that there are gaps in any metal detection system. Even if a metal detector is located at the school's main entranceway, for example, all other doors still have to be staffed and secured to keep out unauthorized people. Ground-level windows have to be secured so no one can slip a weapon through an open window to someone already inside the building. To be effective, metal detectors must be operated full time, twenty-four-hours a day, seven days a week. "It would require

Metal Detectors Are Not the Best Option

Schools have many options for ensuring safety and security—and metal detectors are the least popular of these options, according to a National Institute of Justice study. One reason might be cost; a stationary metal detector suitable for use in a public school costs from $4,000 to $5,000. Most schools have opted for other measures, including controlled access to buildings during school hours, security cameras, and picture IDs for staff and faculty. These and other measures are preferable to metal detectors.

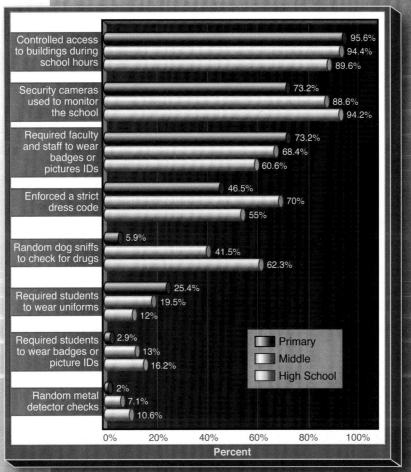

Percentage of Public Schools Using Certain Safety and Security Measures

Measure	Primary	Middle	High School
Controlled access to buildings during school hours	95.6%	94.4%	89.6%
Security cameras used to monitor the school	73.2%	88.6%	94.2%
Required faculty and staff to wear badges or pictures IDs	73.2%	68.4%	60.6%
Enforced a strict dress code	46.5%	70%	55%
Random dog sniffs to check for drugs	5.9%	41.5%	62.3%
Required students to wear uniforms	25.4%	19.5%	12%
Required students to wear badges or picture IDs	2.9%	13%	16.2%
Random metal detector checks	2%	7.1%	10.6%

Percent

Note: Responses were provided by the principal or the person most knowledgeable about crime and safety issues at the school.

Source: National Center for Education Statistics, "School Safety and Security Measures," 2018. https://nces.ed.gov.

an enormous amount of financial, manpower and oversight resources to properly [maintain a metal detection system]," says Trump. "Thus we are pretty confident that there are numerous gaps and holes in implementation of school metal detector programs."[12]

Finally, metal detectors are useless in stopping gun violence that occurs outside a school building on school grounds. "A metal detector would not have prevented the shooting at Townville Elementary in Anderson County on Sept. 28, 2016," notes Paul Powers, a reporter in Charleston, South Carolina, "when a 14-year-old homeschool student allegedly climbed a fence to the playground and opened fire with a handgun."[13] The shooting left one teacher and two children injured, while a third child died from gunshot wounds. Mass shootings can occur in open areas around schools just as easily as in enclosed spaces monitored by metal detectors.

False Sense of Security

Relying too much on metal detectors in schools gives school officials a false sense of security. This misplaced faith in metal detectors can lead teachers and other school personnel to neglect the day-to-day task of looking for possible problems and being alert to signs of violent behavior.

For example, in January 2019 at Burke County Middle School in Georgia, a student managed to sneak a loaded gun into the building despite the school's use of metal detectors. Investigators are not sure how it happened, and no one was hurt, but the incident shows how schools are vulnerable even with metal detectors in place. "You can't have one simple solution that solves [the problem of school shootings]," says Chief Deputy Lewis Blanchard of the Burke County Sheriff's Office. "There is a multitude and layers of things that you have to do and even if it's perfect

> "You can't have one simple solution that solves [the problem of school shootings]. There is a multitude and layers of things that you have to do and even if it's perfect you still can get through."[14]
>
> —Chief Deputy Lewis Blanchard of Georgia's Burke County Sheriff's Office

you still can get through."[14] Instead of spending money and resources on metal detectors, schools should focus on monitoring problem students to keep schools safe.

A Stigma on Urban or Minority Schools

Use of metal detectors can also be a social stigma for schools that are poor, urban, or minority based. Metal detectors tend to promote the idea that the students are prone to violence or must be kept under surveillance. Such an atmosphere can actually reduce students' feelings of trust and safety.

A study by University of Buffalo education professor Jeremy Finn and Canisius College psychology professor Tim Servoss found that safety measures like metal detectors and security cameras are far more likely to be adopted by urban schools with large populations of African American students. In fact, the study showed that African American students are six times more likely than white students to step through a metal detector when entering their school building each morning. The study also found that, despite these heightened security measures, most students felt less safe at school. Instead of promoting better education, the use of metal detectors has a negative effect on teaching and learning. Andrea Colon, a senior at Rockaway Park High School in New York City, sees metal detectors as part of a failed effort to stem violence in schools. Colon asks, "Why are you making the same mistake—prioritizing police and metal detectors—instead of ensuring we have enough social, emotional and mental health support and resources in our schools?"[15]

A Prison-Like Atmosphere

In large schools the use of metal detectors and surveillance cameras can impose a prison-like atmosphere. Students can feel like they are being watched with suspicion instead of protected. As a result, some students are speaking out against the use of metal detectors. In December 2017 several hundred students at Bayard Rustin Educational Complex in New York City protested the sudden installation of metal detectors in their school. They noted that the school across the street, with a higher proportion of white students, did not receive metal detectors. According to Malala Waseme, one of the students who organized the protest, "There was no sense of warning. [The metal detectors] just popped up one day. People felt in a way violated. They see school as their safe space, and to have police officers scanning you, go through your things, it wasn't taken very lightly. Students stopped coming to school because of the anxiety of being surrounded by metal detectors."[16]

> "Why are you making the same mistake—prioritizing police and metal detectors—instead of ensuring we have enough social, emotional and mental health support and resources in our schools?"[15]
>
> —Andrea Colon, a senior at Rockaway Park High School in New York City

Metal detectors are not the answer to stopping school shootings. According to the National Center for Education Statistics, less than 9 percent of high schools in the United States use metal detectors. They are too expensive to be employed widely. They are not reliable at all times, and they tend to give students and teachers alike a false sense of security. Further, the use of metal detectors can stigmatize urban and minority schools by making them seem like prisons prone to violence. Much better solutions should be sought to prevent school shootings in America.

Chapter Two

Should Teachers and Staff Members Be Armed?

Teachers and Staff Members Should Not Be Allowed to Have Guns

- Introducing guns into schools, even for a fraction of teachers and staff members, invites violence.
- Many teachers and staff members do not want to work in schools that allow guns in the classroom or in the building.
- Liability and lawsuits for gun accidents or other gun-related incidents could bankrupt school districts.

The Debate at a Glance

Teachers and Staff Members Should Be Allowed to Have Guns

- A trained person with a gun on-site can prevent a shooting rampage and save lives.
- Making schools into gun-free zones actually encourages shooters to attack without fear of being confronted with a firearm.
- Several states have successfully implemented gun-carry policies for teachers and staff members.

Teachers and Staff Members Should Not Be Allowed to Have Guns

"The overwhelming majority of teachers oppose being armed. Teachers want to be in their classrooms to teach their children. . . . It is incredibly hard to do that when you're packing heat."

—Mary Kusler, senior director of the National Education Association's Center for Advocacy

Quoted in Brandon Griggs and Dakin Andone, "Since Parkland, 14 States Have Introduced 25 Measures to Arm Teachers and Staff. Only 1 Has Passed," CNN, May 21, 2018. www.cnn.com.

Consider these questions as you read:

1. How persuasive is the argument that allowing teachers to be armed in schools would only lead to more violence? Explain your answer.
2. Should teachers and staff members be allowed to make their own decisions on whether to have a gun in school? Why or why not?
3. How important is the issue of liability with regard to the question of arming teachers? Explain.

Editor's note: The discussion that follows presents common arguments made in support of this perspective, reinforced by facts, quotes, and examples taken from various sources.

Teachers and staff members should not have guns in schools. The idea that the scourge of school shootings can be stopped by introducing more guns into schools is ridiculous. The presence of firearms invites violence. This is the reason schools work so hard to keep their halls and classrooms gun-free. The great majority of teachers and school personnel do not want to work in an environment where guns are present, let alone keep firearms themselves. Also, the possibility of gun accidents in schools would lead to lawsuits that could bankrupt school districts that are already struggling. Firearms should be banned from schools entirely—and that includes those in the possession of teachers and school personnel. "The job of an educator is complicated enough," says Starr Sackstein, who has taught in New York City schools for sixteen years. "Adding a firearm to the equation does not equal safety; if anything it adds to the potential danger exponentially."[17]

More Guns Lead to More Violence

Arming teachers and school personnel would only make gun violence in schools more likely to occur. Instead of preventing shootings, the addition of guns would lead to more accidents and tragic errors. Law enforcement experts point out that teachers do not have the training and tactical experience to handle high-stress situations involving firearms. They are more likely to overreact and shoot an innocent person by mistake. Alexis Underwood, a retired US Marine and president of the Association of Bay County Educators, thinks arming teachers is a terrible idea. "One of the things that my drill instructor told me," says Underwood, "is that even individuals in the military, in a moment of crisis, when the gun fires for real, are going to forget what they've been taught to do and they're going to run or they're going to make stupid mistakes."[18] Even if schools had the funds to train their personnel in firearm use—which they do not— teachers carrying concealed weapons in school hallways and classrooms would present an unnecessary risk to students' safety.

Some suggest that firearms could be locked away in a drawer or closet until needed. However, shootings like the one at MSD High School or Santa Fe High School erupt within two or three minutes. There is not enough time for a teacher or administrator to go for the gun and then confront a shooter. Also, a student or unauthorized visitor might find the gun and be tempted to steal it or use it. Dan Staples, a math teacher who served in the US Marine Corps, explains, "First, most of my colleagues have zero interest in carrying. Second, there is a much greater chance of having a negligent discharge or a misplaced weapon or a bad guy getting hold of that weapon than there is of that teacher using it to neutralize a threat."[19]

Introducing a gun into a classroom always involves risks. Just days after the Parkland shooting, a teacher in California who is also a reserve police officer was demonstrating gun safety for his high school class. He accidentally discharged his semiautomatic handgun, shooting a seventeen-year-old student in the neck. Fortunately, the student escaped serious injury. Just before the gun went off, the teacher told the class he was checking to see if it was loaded.

Teachers Want a Gun-Free Environment

When it comes to guns, most teachers in the United States prefer gun control to carrying a gun—or even being around firearms. In fact, a large majority do not want to work in schools in which fellow teachers are allowed to have guns. A Gallup poll of nearly five hundred K–12 teachers found that 73 percent opposed training teachers and other school personnel to carry guns. More than 70 percent believed arming teachers would not help limit casualties in the event of a school shooting. When asked the best method to address school shootings, one-third of the teachers polled said gun control or stricter gun laws. It is obvious that any large-scale attempt to arm teachers is bound to fail miserably. A sizable majority prefer to teach in a gun-free environment, where anxiety about possible gun violence is greatly reduced.

Shortly after the Parkland shooting, President Donald Trump suggested that one remedy is to have certain teachers carry guns. Randi Weingarten, president of the American Federation of Teachers (AFT), responded to Trump with a letter expressing the AFT's opposition to guns in schools. Speaking for the AFT's 1.7 million members, Weingarten told the president, "Schools need to be safe sanctuaries, not armed fortresses. Your

> "First, most of my colleagues have zero interest in carrying. Second, there is a much greater chance of having a negligent discharge or a misplaced weapon or a bad guy getting hold of that weapon than there is of that teacher using it to neutralize a threat."[19]
>
> —Dan Staples, a math teacher who served in the US Marine Corps

Most Teachers Oppose Being Armed at School

According to a Gallup poll conducted in March 2018, 73 percent of US teachers opposed carrying guns in school buildings. A majority of teachers also believed that being armed would not limit the victims in a school shooting and would actually make teachers feel less safe.

Should teachers and staff members carry guns in school buildings?

Strongly favor	Somewhat favor	Neutral	Somewhat oppose	Strongly oppose
11%	9%	7%	10%	63%

If teachers carried guns at your school, how effective would they be in limiting the number of victims in a shooting?

Very effective	Somewhat effective	Not too effective	Not effective at all
13%	16%	24%	47%

How safe would schools be if certain teachers and staff members were armed with guns?

Safer	About as safe as they are now	Less safe
20%	22%	58%

Source: Gallup, "Most U.S. Teachers Oppose Carrying Guns in Schools, March 16, 2018." https://news.gallup.com.

proposal to arm teachers not only would make our children's classrooms less safe, but also is not what educators and students want."[20]

Psychologists note that carrying a firearm or being in an environment where firearms are present creates tension that can affect job performance. Guns can change the way people think and how they look at others. "Being armed places you in a state of mind that is not conducive to teaching," says Joshua Grubbs, a psychology professor at Bowling Green State University and a gun owner himself. "Carrying a firearm responsibly means that you are operating in a state of heightened awareness and caution. You are aware of where your firearm is at all times. You are aware of your environment. You are aware of everyone around you. And whether you want to admit or not, you are looking for a threat."[21] This is not the sort of atmosphere teachers want in our schools.

> "If the teacher panics or doesn't really know how to handle the gun you'll get random fire with them hitting anything or everything."[22]
>
> —Police sergeant Don Cameron of Berkeley, California

Liability and Lawsuits

As a practical matter, arming teachers would present a nightmare of potential legal problems for school districts. This is particularly true in states like California, which have been working to keep all firearms away from school grounds and school personnel. First, any person carrying a gun for security purposes or protection of others has to be certified. This means teachers and staff would have to undergo intensive training with the firearms they carry—more than the ordinary gun owner. Should a teacher who lacked gun certification shoot someone by mistake, the school district could be subject to a huge lawsuit.

Second, armed teachers and staff members would have to abide by the same rules of engagement followed by law enforcement officers. In most jurisdictions, a gun can be fired only to save a life or in urgent self-defense from a shooter or attacker. Failure to abide by these rules would again leave the school district open to a lawsuit. As Berkeley, California, police sergeant Don Cameron observes, "If the teacher panics or doesn't really know how to handle the gun you'll get random fire with them hitting anything or everything."[22]

Third, guns at school would have to be stored securely in a firearms locker or other safe place. Should a student or other unauthorized person steal a weapon and harm someone with it, the school district could be sued for negligence. With school districts around the country facing a funding crisis, inviting new legal problems by arming teachers is a terrible idea.

Those in favor of arming teachers like to say it takes a good person with a gun to stop a bad person with a gun. However, this oversimplifies the issue of allowing teachers and school staff members to have guns. Introducing more guns into schools only increases the chances of violent incidents and accidental shootings. The overwhelming majority of teachers prefer to work in schools that are gun-free. And arming teachers leaves school districts open to huge lawsuits should a student or visitor be shot by mistake. The best way to keep America's students safe is to keep guns out of schools—including out of the hands of teachers.

Teachers and Staff Members Should Be Allowed to Have Guns

"Preventing trained teachers from being able to defend their lives and their students has proven to be a bad idea. . . . Allowing trained staff to be armed and carry concealed weapons on campus is the best short-term solution."

—Joseph T. Drammissi, board member of San Diego County Gun Owners

Joseph T. Drammissi, "Commentary: Should Teachers Be Armed? Yes: Staff Can Keep Students Safe," *San Diego Union-Tribune*, February 28, 2018. www.sandiegouniontribune.org.

Consider these questions as you read:

1. Do you think school districts are justified in preventing teachers and staff members from being armed? Explain your answer.
2. How persuasive is the argument that making schools into gun-free zones leaves them vulnerable to school shooters? Explain your answer.
3. Do you agree that student anxiety about a gun attack is eased when teachers are armed? Why or why not?

Editor's note: The discussion that follows presents common arguments made in support of this perspective, reinforced by facts, quotes, and examples taken from various sources.

Time and again, when a mass shooting occurs in the United States, people will observe that so many lives could have been saved if only someone at the scene had been armed and able to stop the shooter. This is no different with the school shootings at MSD High School in Parkland, Florida, and Santa Fe High School in Houston, Texas. Law enforcement cannot possibly respond quickly enough to prevent these tragedies. We need school policies that allow teachers and staff members to carry or have access to guns in case of an emergency. Administrators should encourage teachers to get firearms training and become licensed to carry. Attempts to turn American schools into gun-free zones actually make them less safe by letting potential shooters know they will not face someone with a firearm. Some states already have implemented successful gun-carry policies for teachers, and more are going forward with plans of their own. It is foolish to deny teachers and staff members the right to arm themselves in order to defend their students from a rampaging shooter.

Teachers with Guns Can Save Lives

The only way to stop an armed attacker inside a school building or on school grounds is for another person with a gun to step up and take action. That is why teachers and staff members must be allowed to have guns in schools. A teacher on-site that is trained to use a firearm can bring down a shooter in an emergency. For defenseless students, it can be a matter of life and death.

Those who are opposed to allowing teachers to be armed often are against gun ownership altogether. They believe teachers carrying guns somehow creates an atmosphere of fear and anxiety, when the opposite is more likely the case. If students know that a shooter will quickly be confronted by armed teachers or staff members trained to use their weapons, they will have less fears of a deadly shooting spree in their school. Other anti-gun voices insist that arming teachers will cause more gun violence in schools. Apparently, they think teachers cannot be trusted with firearms. However, as Daniel Payne, a Virginia-based blogger and magazine editor, observes, "Concealed carriers are among the most law-abiding individuals in the country. And schools could insist on strict safety protocols for teachers who carry: training, certification, a careful and deliberate system of ensuring that guns remain where they're supposed to be at all times."[23]

The Problem with Gun-Free Zones

Anti-gun activists tout the idea of gun-free zones as an obvious way to stop school shootings. But the push to maintain schools as gun-free zones actually can invite gun violence. Shooters know they can carry out an attack without anyone shooting back. Only by arming teachers and other personnel can schools change that equation. Potential attackers should know that schools are no longer so-called soft targets with no means of defense. And FBI statistics show that shooters almost always either surrender or shoot themselves if confronted by someone with a gun. "Would you put a gun-free zone sticker or yard sign in front of your house?" asks Whitney Blake, a journalist in Washington, DC. "No, you put up signs indicating you have a security system."[24]

Finally, some believe that the only exceptions to gun-free zones in schools should be professional security officers or part-time police officers, not armed teachers or staff members. Yet professional guards are expensive to hire, and they cannot be everywhere in a school building should violence erupt. Moreover, recent history shows that even professionals can fall short in a crisis. In the Parkland, Florida, shooting, the armed deputy whose job it was to protect the school chose not to enter the building as students were being murdered. He crouched behind a pillar outside for forty-five minutes. A teacher with a gun likely would have been far more effective.

> "Would you put a gun-free zone sticker or yard sign in front of your house? No, you put up signs indicating you have a security system."[24]
>
> —Whitney Blake, a journalist in Washington, DC

Successful Gun-Carry Policies for Teachers

Several states have responded to school shootings by setting up policies that allow teachers to carry firearms. Despite predictions of disaster from gun control advocates, these programs have been notably successful. Such programs demonstrate that arming teachers and staff members can promote school safety and provide peace of mind for students.

The Gun-Free School Zones Act, passed in 1990, is a federal law that generally prohibits having firearms within 1,000 feet (305 m) of a school zone. However, the law does not apply to adults with permits to carry a concealed gun. At least ten states, including Illinois, Michigan, New

A Growing Number of States Allow Teachers to Carry Guns

Across the United States, many state legislatures and school districts allow teachers to be armed in public schools. This reflects the belief that teachers with guns can help prevent a school shooting or other acts of violence.

Teachers in at least one school district are armed

State law permits school districts to arm teachers

Legislation to arm teachers is pending

States that do not allow teachers to have guns in schools

Source: Vice News/National Council of State Legislatures/Giffords Law Center, "Here's All the States Where Teachers Already Carry Guns in the Classroom," March 10, 2018. https://news.vice.com.

Hampshire, and Oregon—not exactly strongholds of gun fanatics—have passed laws allowing adults with permits to carry a concealed firearm on school property.

Twenty-five states allow school districts and school boards to decide whether teachers and staff members can be armed. For example, in the wake of the 2018 Parkland shootings, Florida set up a $67 million school marshal program to train and arm teachers. School districts in Texas have implemented concealed-carry policies for their teachers and administrators for more than a decade. According to Texas governor Greg Abbott, pro-gun school districts are not shy about their policies. "Candidly, some school districts, they promote it," says Abbott. "Because they will have signs out front—a warning sign: 'Be aware, there are armed personnel on campus'—warning anybody coming on there that they—if they attempt to cause any harm, they're going to be in trouble."[25]

Successful gun-carry policies are found in schools throughout the country. The Clarksville School District, located 100 miles (161 km) northwest of Little Rock, Arkansas, has had an open-carry policy since 2015. Instead of hiring an extra full-time security guard for about $50,000 per year, the district has spent $68,000 to train thirteen teachers and staff members in firearm safety. Each year, they undergo further training, including active shooter drills in the hallways after hours. Having these armed personnel ready to respond in an emergency eases the fears of both students and teachers. Jim Krohn, a social studies teacher at Clarksville Junior High, volunteered for the program and believes in its effectiveness. "If we didn't do this and somebody came into this building or any of our school buildings and harmed children, it would be hard to go to sleep that night thinking what else could I have done," says Krohn, "and at least we've done what we think is the best thing to protect the children of Clarksville school district."[26]

After the MSD High School and Santa Fe High School shootings, several districts in South Dakota applied to join a school sentinel program, to provide volunteer teachers and staff members training in firearms safety and emergency response. Before participants can begin the eighty-hour training program, they must be approved by their school

"If we didn't [allow teachers to be armed] and somebody came into this building or any of our school buildings and harmed children, it would be hard to go to sleep that night thinking what else could I have done."[26]

—Jim Krohn, a social studies teacher at Clarksville Junior High in Arkansas district and local law enforcement. They also must get a physical exam to show they are able to perform the required duties. The program is especially valuable in isolated rural districts in states like South Dakota, where precious minutes go by before police can arrive in an emergency.

In spite of fears by anti-gun activists, teachers and school personnel should be allowed to arm themselves. In a potential mass shooting incident, only a trained person on-site with a gun can confront a shooter and protect students. Attempts to create so-called gun-free zones in schools, and thus prevent teachers from being armed, can actually lead shooters to think they can stage an attack with no fear of confronting a firearm. And far from being dangerous, gun-carry policies in school districts across the nation have been remarkably successful. Unreasonable fears about guns should not keep schools from allowing teachers and other staff members to be armed and ready to respond in a crisis.

Chapter Three

Should Schools Have Mental Health Counseling Programs?

Schools Should Not Have Mental Health Counseling Programs

- Creating school programs for mental health counseling would not prevent school shootings.
- Students who receive counseling for mental health at school may be stigmatized by teachers and shunned by other students, thus contributing to the problem.
- Decisions about mental health counseling should be left to a student's parents or guardian.

The Debate at a Glance

Schools Should Have Mental Health Counseling Programs

- A mental health counseling program at school can help prevent a tragedy by offering professional help to students who show signs of being at risk for violence.
- Public school systems can partner with community mental health agencies to create cost-effective school programs.
- A school mental health counseling program can encourage students, teachers, and staff members to report early warning signs, knowing the individual can get help instead of facing detention or jail.

Schools Should Not Have Mental Health Counseling Programs

"The familiar narrative whereby calls for better mental health crop up immediately after a mass murder is unhelpful in solving the gun violence crisis, and it may do more harm than good for the mentally ill."

—Noam Shpancer, a professor of psychology at Otterbein University in Westerville, Ohio

Noam Shpancer, "Improved Mental Health Care Won't Prevent Mass Shootings," *Psychology Today*, March 27, 2018. www.psychologytoday.com.

Consider these questions as you read:

1. What is the strongest argument for the view that mental health programs in schools would not help prevent school shootings? Explain your answer.
2. How can schools deal with the stigma attached to students who receive mental health counseling?
3. Do you agree that decisions about mental health counseling should be left to the student's parents or guardian? Why or why not?

Editor's note: The discussion that follows presents common arguments made in support of this perspective, reinforced by facts, quotes, and examples taken from various sources.

In the aftermath of school shootings, many people try to change the subject from gun control to mental health. And inevitably someone will demand that schools provide mental health counseling services. Schools are not the place for this. Turning schools into psychiatric clinics in order to spot troubled individuals who might be prone to violence is a foolish waste of time and resources. Mental health counseling at schools would not prevent school shootings. Such incidents are typically the product of loneliness, rage, and an attachment to firearms, and not actual mental illness. Treating students at school for psychiatric problems would stigmatize them among their classmates and might lead them to feel alienated. Decisions about mental health treatment should be left to parents and guardians, rather than taken over by school authorities. It is time to abandon the idea that schools can safeguard themselves against gun violence by spending scarce resources on mental health counseling.

Limits of Mental Health Counseling

Calls for schools to focus on mental health care to prevent school shootings are misguided. American families no doubt would benefit from better mental health policies. But placing more psychologists in schools would likely have zero effect on school shootings. Many of the characteristics of those who have committed mass shootings in schools are commonplace among young people. Anger, resentment, loneliness, inadequacy, and alienation are felt by many teenagers to one degree or another. These are hardly the signs of mental illness. As Noam Shpancer, a professor of psychology at Otterbein University in Westerville, Ohio, observes, "In fact, factors other than mental illness are far better predictors of gun violence, including being male, using drugs and alcohol, a history of childhood abuse, and, of course, the availability of guns."[27]

> "This is one of the greatest dilemmas of psychologists and parents: How can they possibly tell in advance who is a real threat and who isn't?"[28]
>
> —Barbara Bradley Hagerty, a journalist writing on school shootings and troubled children

Mental health counselors cannot see into the future, which they would have to do in order to identify a student who is on the verge of committing mass murder. "Of course, the vast majority of children post or say threatening things and never act on them," says Barbara Bradley Hagerty, who has written about school shootings and troubled children. "This is one of the greatest dilemmas of psychologists and parents: How can they possibly tell in advance who is a real threat and who isn't?"[28]

Parents Question Schools' Ability to Deal with Mental Health Issues

Parents are much less confident that their child's school can deal with mental health issues compared to other health problems such as first aid or an asthma attack. Mental health counseling at public schools does not inspire confidence that it can prevent mentally ill students from committing violent acts.

Percentage of Parents Who Are Very Confident

	Elementary School	Middle/High School
Give first aid	84%	70%
Respond to an asthma attack	63%	54%
Assist with suspected mental health problems	45%	32%

Source: Mott Poll Report, "Handling Child Health Needs During the School Day," September 18, 2017. https://mottpoll.org.

Sometimes there are almost no indications of trouble. A good example is seventeen-year-old Dimitrios Pagourtzis, whose shooting rampage at Houston's Santa Fe High School left ten dead and ten wounded. Prior to the attack, Pagourtzis showed few signs of violent behavior. He was quiet and reserved. He played on the football team, made the honor roll, and thought about joining the US Marines. He had never been arrested or had run-ins with police. He liked to play violent video games, but certainly that is not unusual among teens. Pagourtzis's journal entries about killing people were not discovered until after he had carried his father's shotgun and .38 revolver into the high school and opened fire on classmates. According to Texas governor Greg Abbott, "The red-flag warnings were either nonexistent or very imperceptible."[29]

Hiring an army of mental health professionals or social workers in America's schools would require spending large sums for meager results. These funds would be subtracted from school budgets that are already inadequate. In 2017 Wisconsin's legislature increased spending for school mental health services by $6.5 million, yet experts said the sum was too small to address the state's needs. A better plan is to encourage teachers, parents, and classmates to be alert to unusual or aggressive behavior in their daily interactions with youths. This practical approach beats turning schools into psychiatric wards.

Stigma of Treatment for Troubled Youths

Treating students for mental illness in schools can actually stigmatize them among their classmates. This in turn can increase their feelings of depression and alienation. Mental health experts stress that just the opposite needs to occur. Troubled young people desperately need to feel like part of a community. They need to build self-esteem. They benefit most from being surrounded by people who care about them. Unfortunately, however, many people think of mental illness as something to be feared. The public often links it with violent behavior, despite statistics showing that people with mental illness are far more likely to be the victims of violence than the perpetrators of it. "The stereotype about violence and mental illness is not just inaccurate; it is dangerous," says Jonathan Foiles, a therapist at a community mental health clinic in Chicago. "Every story that suggests a causal link between mental illness and violence increases the stigma of having a mental illness, making it less likely that those experiencing a mental illness will seek help."[30]

Bringing mental health counselors into schools could backfire in

> "Every story that suggests a causal link between mental illness and violence increases the stigma of having a mental illness, making it less likely that those experiencing a mental illness will seek help."[30]
>
> —Jonathan Foiles, a therapist at a community mental health clinic in Chicago

many ways. Thousands of troubled students display characteristics that fit the clichéd profile of a shooter. The vast majority are harmless and innocent. Yet they could end up being labeled as problem children who have to be watched. They could be forced into mental hospitals or treatment centers. Their freedoms could be curtailed in the interests of school safety. Such treatment would only increase their resentment and paranoid feelings toward society. Meanwhile, those few students capable of deadly violence tend to avoid counseling and keep their thoughts to themselves. "[Mass shooters] are unlikely to trust a therapist who insists on self-reflection and unlikely to confess to their true plans and fantasies," says Shpancer. "For those who plan to carry out mass murder, staying off the mental health system radar, refusing help, and denying illness are bound to be preferred strategies."[31]

Leave Mental Health Decisions to Parents

Preventing school shootings is a vital goal, yet the effort should not override parents' rights to make decisions about their children. The rush to blame school shootings on mental illness has many parents worried about labeling and clumsy interventions. For example, after the Parkland shootings, the Florida legislature quickly passed a law requiring children to answer questions about their mental health when registering for school. Every school district in the state must now find out whether a child has ever been referred for mental health treatment.

Florida's new policy worries many parents. They are leery of their children being labeled throughout their school careers. They also resist the idea of school authorities getting involved in personal decisions. "If you do say, 'Yes, my child has seen a counselor or a therapist or a psychologist,' what does the school then do with that?"[32] asks Laura Goodhue, who has a nine-year-old with autism and a ten-year-old who has been treated by a psychologist. Such policies are not just an overreaction; they are an attack on privacy rights and personal freedom. They show how, if the government continues to expand mental health counseling in schools, parental concerns could be brushed aside in favor of school priorities.

Despite the trauma of school shootings in Florida and Texas, mental illness should not be linked to mass murder. Placing mental health counselors in schools will not prevent mass shootings. Psychologists cannot possibly predict which troubled students might commit a murderous act. Mental health screening in schools might actually make things worse by stigmatizing troubled youths and alienating them from classmates. Also, these policies threaten to affect parents' ability to make decisions about their children's care. School districts should consider these factors before expanding mental health care in schools.

Schools Should Have Mental Health Counseling Programs

"Imagine the shootings we may be able to avoid if teachers could be trained of warning signs and mental health staff was available to put a safety and success plan in place including counseling."

—Tricia K. Daniel, president of the Alabama Association of School Psychologists

Tricia K. Daniel, "Fight School Shootings with Mental Health Care, Not Guns," AL.com, June 27, 2018. www.al.com.

Consider these questions as you read:

1. How persuasive is the argument that a school mental health program can help prevent school shooting incidents? Explain your answer.
2. Do you believe the federal government should provide funding for mental health programs in all schools? Why or why not?
3. What problems could arise from enlisting teachers and staff members to report early warning signs of violent behavior in students?

Editor's note: The discussion that follows presents common arguments made in support of this perspective, reinforced by facts, quotes, and examples taken from various sources.

Schools in the United States desperately need mental health counseling programs to screen for youths with psychological problems. This would help prevent school shootings by identifying troubled students with violent tendencies before a tragedy occurs. School districts that partner with community mental health agencies can create school programs that are affordable and effective. And having a mental health program at school can actually prompt teachers and students to report warning signs for at-risk youths, knowing that an individual will not be punished or institutionalized but instead can undergo counseling. It is time that American schools recognize the need to promote mental health as part of their educational mission. According to Nancy Barile, an award-winning teacher at an urban school near Boston, Massachusetts, "Mental health awareness is an important issue for all educators, who are often the first line of defense for their students."[33]

Mental Health Counseling Programs Can Prevent Shootings

One of the best ways to prevent school shootings is to set up mental health care programs in schools. Identifying a possibly violent youth calls for regular contact and an eye for early warning signs. Schools are excellent sites for prevention, intervention, and positive feedback. Those that employ or provide access to psychologists, counselors, social workers, and school nurses can offer help to troubled young people in a familiar setting. States are starting to recognize the importance of school-based mental health programs. In the wake of the Parkland school shootings, the Florida legislature allocated millions of dollars for mental health counselors and services in central Florida schools. "This is what we've been begging for," says Kristine Landry, an educational psychologist and director of student services for Lake County Schools. "I know it's because of this great tragedy, but if it helps to bring these mental health services to the schools, we can make those deaths mean something."[34]

Research shows that when mental health care is offered at school, teens are more likely to seek counseling. School-based counseling for mental health has the potential to head off violence and increase student safety, not to mention improve academic performance and lower dropout rates. "We're finding that young people are more eager to talk about these issues," says Theresa Nguyen, vice president of policy and programs at Mental Health America. "They hunger for this type of support and conversation and are looking to their school to provide it."[35]

In today's stressful world, young people need access to mental health counseling more than ever. The US Department of Health and Human Services reports that one in five children and adolescents in the United

States experience a problem with mental health during their school years. Adolescents cope with stress, anxiety, depression, bullying, family problems, learning disabilities, and substance abuse, among other problems. For young people, serious mental health problems are on the increase, including self-injury and thoughts of suicide. Yet lack of access to proper care means that an estimated 60 percent of students fail to get the treatment they need. As Katie Hurley, who worked for years as a school-based therapist, notes:

> I saw firsthand how powerful the presence of staff therapists can be. Children who needed weekly sessions were able to access their therapist on campus during the school day. Those who simply needed a safe landing place on a tough day always had someone to listen. Sometimes I entered classrooms to teach social skills lessons or to help with test anxiety by leading the kids in deep-breathing exercises.[36]

Efforts to connect with students on a regular basis can make all the difference in keeping schools safe from violence. Mental health professionals, backed by teachers and school staff, are able to reach out to troubled students. They can spot warning signs that a student is becoming a danger to him- or herself or to others. This might be the best answer—short of widespread gun control—to stop school shootings in the future.

"I saw firsthand how powerful the presence of staff therapists can be. Children who needed weekly sessions were able to access their therapist on campus during the school day."[36]

—Katie Hurley, a former school-based mental health therapist

Partnering with Community Mental Health Agencies

Critics of school-based mental health programs often claim they cost too much for most school districts to maintain. Strapped for funding, many districts cannot afford to hire more than one or two therapists or counselors to cover all their schools. The National Association of School

Mental Illness More Common as Students Reach Adolescence

As students grow older, they become more susceptible to mental health problems such as depression and anxiety. This demonstrates the need for mental health counseling in public schools.

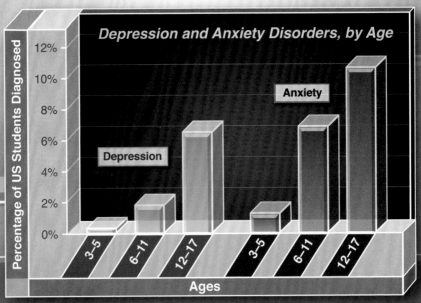

Source: Centers for Disease Control and Prevention, "Facts About Mental Disorders in U.S. Children," December 20, 2018. www.cdc.gov.

Psychologists recommends that school districts have one psychologist for every five hundred to seven hundred students. However, as critics point out, the ratio in many districts is one to one thousand or even fifteen hundred, thus reducing the program's effectiveness. Some districts have no funds for mental health care at all.

To deal with the shortage of school-based mental health professionals, schools are trying new approaches that are both effective and affordable. School districts are partnering with community mental health agencies to meet their students' needs for professional help. Instead of hiring full-time counselors at individual schools, a district can set up regular visits by psychologists. These professionals can screen students for problems such as stress, anxiety, anger issues, or substance abuse. Some schools rely on a school nurse or social worker to help with the screening. Once a student's needs have been identified and parents' permission obtained, the student can be referred to a mental health specialist at a local agency. Some schools have had success connecting students to a therapist by video conference, which is even more cost effective. In interviews with troubled students, a psychologist can probe for warning signs of violent behavior. In a 2017 report for the American Institutes for Research, authors Elizabeth Freeman and Kimberly Kendziora state:

> Partnerships between schools and community mental/behavioral health professionals offer students and families an extended network of services that are easily accessible. When programs are able to identify and address student mental and behavioral challenges early, students are more likely to . . . be successful in school and life while the threat of later harm is reduced.[37]

Getting Help Instead of Punishment or Jail

A school-based mental health program is more likely to produce better outcomes for troubled students. Those who exhibit sudden violent tendencies or act out in class could easily wind up in the juvenile justice system. Too often, this system is a pipeline to prison and long-term failure. However, a school-based program can enlist psychologists, social workers, counselors, teachers, staff members, and even other students to get help for these individuals. People might not hesitate to report unusual or threatening behavior if they believe the offender will receive sympathetic treatment and not be automatically expelled or turned over to police. In this way all levels of the school system can work together to help students who show signs of mental

> "Schools sometimes serve as the de facto [actual] mental health system for children in the United States."[38]
>
> —Authors Elizabeth Freeman and Kimberly Kendziora in a 2017 report for the American Institutes for Research

illness. As Freeman and Kendziora note in their report, "Schools some-times serve as the de facto [actual] mental health system for children in the United States."[38] In poor school districts and rural areas, a school-based program may be the only mental health outlet students ever see. That is all the more reason such programs should be aimed at treatment, not punishment, for potentially violent students.

Arguments against setting up mental health counseling programs in schools ring hollow in light of the school shootings in recent years. School-based mental health programs can screen for signs that a student is at risk to commit violent acts. This can head off a potential tragedy. Cost is an important consideration, but partnering with outside mental health agencies and enlisting school staff for support can be cost effective. And school-based programs can focus on getting help for troubled students, instead of punishing them or placing them in institutions. With all these benefits in mind, it is clear that all schools should have some form of mental health program in place.

Chapter Four

Does Media Coverage Contribute to the School Shootings Problem?

Media Coverage Contributes to the School Shootings Problem

- Widespread media coverage helps perpetrators achieve the fame they are seeking.
- Media coverage can lead disturbed individuals to engage in copycat behavior.
- Reporting in detail the way that a school shooter evaded security could encourage another individual to employ the same method.

The Debate at a Glance

Media Coverage Does Not Contribute to the School Shootings Problem

- The news media has a responsibility to cover major stories like school shootings, and the public has a right to know about these tragedies.
- Reporting on school shootings can bring about policy changes to help prevent such incidents in the future.
- Blaming the media for school shootings is an attempt to shift responsibility away from people's own failures in dealing with the problem.

Media Coverage Contributes to the School Shootings Problem

"[School shooters] are explicitly seeking fame, and the media is helping them to achieve this end."

—Jaclyn Schildkraut, assistant professor in the Department of Public Justice at the State University of New York at Oswego

Jaclyn Schildkraut, "The Media Should Stop Making School Shooters Famous," Vox, March 31, 2018. www.vox.com.

Consider these questions as you read:

1. Can media outlets cover school shootings without giving the offenders the notoriety they seek? Explain your answer.
2. Do you believe the copycat effect in school shootings is the media's fault? Why or why not?
3. What are the pros and cons of focusing on school security systems in media coverage of school shootings? Explain your answer.

Editor's note: The discussion that follows presents common arguments made in support of this perspective, reinforced by facts, quotes, and examples taken from various sources.

The public's interest in shocking events such as the 2018 school shootings in Parkland, Florida, and Houston, Texas, is understandable. Yet media coverage of school shootings only makes the problem worse. When TV networks and newspapers repeat perpetrators' names over and over for days on end, the media are providing shooters with the fame they were seeking. Making an instant celebrity out of a mass murderer can lead other troubled teens to contemplate a similar attack. Moreover, reporting in detail how a school shooter managed to evade security and carry out a killing spree might enable future shooters to do the same. Weighing the public's right to know with the potential dangers of too much coverage

The Media Must Limit Coverage to Avoid Copycat Shootings

Academic studies show that extensive media coverage of mass shootings can trigger copycat behavior in someone who is already deeply troubled and predisposed to violence. To keep this from happening, researchers and others have proposed voluntary limits on media coverage of mass shootings, including those that occur in schools.

Guidelines for Media Reporting in Cases of Mass Shootings

1. Do not name the perpetrator.

2. Do not use photos or likenesses of the perpetrator.

3. Stop using the names, photos, or likenesses of past perpetrators.

4. Report everything else about these crimes in as much detail as desired.

Source: NRA-ILA, "Media Contagion Effect and Mass Shootings," January 11, 2019. www.nraila.org.

is difficult. But today's media need to realize the power they wield. They should refrain from doing anything to glamorize these horrifying crimes.

Do Not Give School Shooters the Attention They Seek

It cannot be denied that widespread coverage of school shootings bestows fame on the perpetrators. And often this is exactly what they want. It may be the main reason most school shooters commit their criminal acts. They generally are alienated young people harboring rage and resentment against a world that ignores them. They are inspired by the thought of all the attention their murderous sprees will attract. By making these shooters into household names, the media become complicit in helping them achieve their purpose. For this reason, it is time for TV networks, newspapers, and other media outlets to rethink the way they cover school shootings. The media should refuse to name or show pictures of school shooters and deny them the notoriety they are seeking. Lobbying groups such as Don't Name Them and No Notoriety are already having success in convincing news outlets to focus more on the victims than offenders in these crimes.

In the days following the school shootings at MSD High School and Santa Fe High School, the public learned a great deal about the young men responsible for these attacks. Media reports about Nikolas Cruz, the Parkland shooter, detailed his frequent run-ins with authorities, his racial abuse of black students, his carving of swastikas on his school desk, and his habit of bringing dead animals to school and waving them in other students' faces. Broward County prosecutors also released a cell phone video Cruz posted to social media shortly before his killing spree. Brandishing a rifle, Cruz says to the camera, "When you see me on the news, you'll all know who I am. You're all going to die. . . . Yeah, can't wait."[39] The video appeared on dozens of news outlets and received millions of hits on YouTube. However, students at MSD High School protested how the media publicized the video. "So can people please not spread that video around," tweeted Morgan Williams, a Parkland student. "It is only giving him what he wants."[40] A few news organizations, such as CBS News, chose not to broadcast or publish the video. The Daily Wire announced it would no longer publish the names or pictures of those responsible for any future attacks.

Erica Goode, formerly a reporter for the *New York Times*, noticed a new restraint in coverage of Cruz and the Parkland shootings. Yet the story still went through the typical cycle for such traumatic national events. "You do the day story, and then you do the victim stories, and then you profile the shooter," says Goode. But as she points out, "A profile of the shooter is not going to help anybody understand who these people are. It's going to make them famous, basically."[41] Goode

> "A profile of the shooter is not going to help anybody understand who these people are. It's going to make them famous, basically."[41]
>
> —Erica Goode, a former reporter for the *New York Times*

was pleased that much of the Parkland coverage pivoted to focus on the victims and their families as well as possible solutions to the problem of school shootings.

The Danger of Copycat Behavior

Extensive news coverage of school shootings brings with it the danger of copycat behavior—or *contagion*, as researchers call it. That is when stories about an event such as a school shooting influence some other troubled, at-risk youth to commit the same kind of violent act. It has long been suspected that mentally unstable persons thinking about mass murder might be tipped into acting by a deluge of reports about a similar crime. Police in particular have noted this chain reaction.

Researchers at Arizona State University and Northeastern Illinois University say the concern about copycat behavior has a firm basis in statistics. Using data compiled from the Brady Campaign to Prevent Gun Violence and FBI reports, they found that up to 30 percent of attacks are triggered by other attacks. The effect appears to last about thirteen days after a well-publicized incident. This is easily within the window of blanket news coverage for recent school shootings. "The copycat phenomenon is real," says Andre Simons of the FBI's Behavioral Analysis Unit. "As more and more notable and tragic events occur, we think we're seeing more compromised, marginalized individuals who are seeking inspiration from those past attacks."[42]

> "The copycat phenomenon is real. As more and more notable and tragic events occur, we think we're seeing more compromised, marginalized individuals who are seeking inspiration from those past attacks."[42]
>
> —Andre Simons of the FBI's Behavioral Analysis Unit

After the shootings at Santa Fe High School, several survivors admitted they had almost come to expect an attack. "It's been happening everywhere," says Paige Curry, a student at Santa Fe. "I've always kind of felt like eventually it was going to happen here."[43] Widespread fears about copycat behavior are another reason why news outlets should rethink their policies on covering school shootings. Their reports may inspire other teenagers to go on a shooting rampage.

Inadvertently Helping Future Shooters

News coverage of school shootings may help other potential shooters plan an attack. Detailed reports of how a shooter obtained weapons or managed to evade school security can encourage other unstable youths to follow the same blueprint. Allowing the public to see surveillance video of a school attack provides a step-by-step course in how to stage an armed attack. Even reporting on how schools intend to prevent school shootings may assist a future shooter. The media should consider these dangers to avoid making the problem worse.

For example, Nikolas Cruz benefited from his knowledge of the security system at MSD High School. As a former student there, he knew about the school's active shooter drills and how staff members and other students would react. In the days after the massacre, media reports detailed how Cruz got through security gates and used the fire alarm to create chaos. These reports certainly could be useful to a copycat attacker. According to William Cummings, who covered the Parkland shootings for *USA Today*, "It is common for the attackers who commit mass shootings to make detailed plans ahead of the event and to search for lessons to be drawn from other attacks."[44] The media must avoid helping the next school shooter carry out a successful attack.

There is little doubt that most school shooters seek to become famous—or notorious. With this in mind, media coverage should avoid naming the shooters or displaying their pictures. Limiting media coverage of school shootings would also help solve the problem of copycat attackers who are inspired by news reports. In addition, the media should rethink their role in publicizing school security plans and helping a future attacker evade them. In a free society the media must balance the public's right to know with practical considerations about not glorifying school shooters.

Media Coverage Does Not Contribute to the School Shootings Problem

"For each individual story, we must consider what is newsworthy. In [the Parkland case] the videos help readers better understand the life and thinking of the accused killer, which is relevant to his prosecution."

—A spokesperson for the *Washington Post*

Quoted in Kelly-Leigh Cooper, "Does the Media Have a Problem with Coverage of Mass Shootings?," BBC, May 31, 2018. www.bbc.com.

Consider these questions as you read:

1. Do you agree that the public's right to know justifies extensive news coverage of school shootings? Why or why not?
2. Should the media stress gun control and gun rights issues in their coverage of school shootings? Why or why not?
3. Do you believe the media cover school shootings in a fair manner? Explain your answer.

Editor's note: The discussion that follows presents common arguments made in support of this perspective, reinforced by facts, quotes, and examples taken from various sources.

With regard to news coverage of school shootings, it is foolish to blame the messenger. The media do not make the problem of school shootings worse. News organizations are merely doing their job in covering these tragic stories because the public has both a right and a need to know. Such reporting actually can be beneficial, helping bring about policy changes that can prevent such attacks in the future. Criticisms of the media are understandable when survivors and their families want less attention focused on the individuals who carry out these terrible massacres. Often, however, these criticisms attempt to shift blame from authorities who failed to stop the shootings in the first place. It is important to recognize that the media are focused on keeping people informed, which is vital in a democracy.

Responsibility to Keep People Informed

The news media do not create the school shootings problem. Reporters investigate these attacks because they are newsworthy, and people want to know how and why they occur. In fact the media have a responsibility to keep people informed about such terrible events. Only by getting the facts about school shootings can people make judgments about how society, including law enforcement and school authorities, should respond.

Critics and activists who claim that gun attacks in schools are partly caused by news media are misguided. It is like saying that wars would cease if reporters declined to cover them. This is a simplistic reaction to an emotional issue. "Members of the media can't simply bury their heads in the sand whenever a madman opens fire in an American school," says reporter Jared Keller. "Media organizations have an ethical responsibility to bear witness to the tragedies of history, to ensure that future generations don't forget the horrors of epochs [times] past."[45]

> "Media organizations have an ethical responsibility to bear witness to the tragedies of history, to ensure that future generations don't forget the horrors of epochs [times] past."[45]
>
> —Jared Keller, news reporter

Lobbying groups like No Notoriety seek to convince news outlets to adopt rigid policies about not naming school shooters or providing personal information about them. But producers, editors, and reporters have to remain independent in making these decisions. They must make judgment calls on how to profile a shooter, balancing sensitivity toward victims with the public's right to know. For example, after the Parkland shootings, prosecutors in Florida released a controversial cell phone video made by

The Media Must Fully Cover All School Shootings

On May 18, 2018, the three major cable news networks devoted only a limited amount of coverage time to the school shootings at Santa Fe High School in Houston, Texas. If anything, the coverage should have been more extensive. Americans need to understand the full extent of what is taking place in the nation's schools. Anything less than that will leave them with a false sense that all is well when it is not.

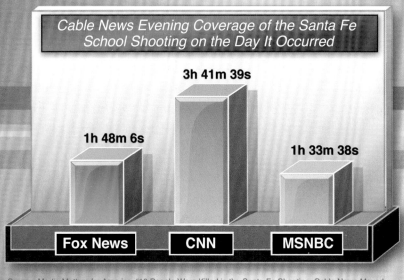

Cable News Evening Coverage of the Santa Fe School Shooting on the Day It Occurred

1h 48m 6s	3h 41m 39s	1h 33m 38s
Fox News	CNN	MSNBC

Source: Media Matters for America, "10 People Were Killed in the Santa Fe Shooting. Cable News Moved on Almost Immediately," May 25, 2018. www.mediamatters.org.

Nikolas Cruz not long before he entered the school building. The video, with Cruz cold-bloodedly declaring his intention to murder as many of his former classmates as possible, is certainly disturbing, even disgusting. But it is hard to argue it did not have news value. Some news organizations refused to broadcast the video, although a majority did present it with warnings about the video's chilling content. Seeing it helped people understand the background of the shooter. It also placed the attack in context. "It shows premeditation," says Penny Brill, former head of the Miami-Dade State Attorney's Office. "It wasn't a spur of the moment decision to shoot."[46] Details about how an attack was planned and carried out are crucial elements in covering the news and keeping the public informed.

News Coverage Can Influence

Some critics argue that news organizations should show *more* details about school shootings, not fewer. They contend that if the public saw scenes of murdered children lying in blood-spattered hallways, they might be spurred to demand action about school safety and gun control. In an interview about the 2012 school shootings at Sandy Hook Elementary, former US Attorney General Eric Holder declared, "If the American people had access to those pictures, if the American people had seen those pictures, the calls for reasonable gun safety measures would have passed."[47] *Slate* reporter Jamelle Bouie agrees there could be benefits from more graphic news reports:

> For all of the [mass shootings], though, it's striking how little Americans have actually seen of the violence. We are shown the aftermath, and sometimes—as with Parkland—we see victims hiding or escaping. But we don't see what the bullets actually do. We don't see the crumpled bodies or the bloody hallways, the mutilation that results when a medium-caliber round leaves a high-powered rifle and strikes a living person. . . . That might be part of the problem. . . . Maybe we need to *see* the results of our choices—of our policies—to prompt a change.[48]

A similar argument could be made about the public release of Cruz's cell phone video. Seeing it, a person might question why such a dangerous young person is legally able to obtain a firearm. Suppressing the video would have left out an important aspect of the Parkland story. Certainly, it is important to show sensitivity toward the feelings of victims' family members and the young

"For all of the [mass shootings], though, it's striking how little Americans have actually seen of the violence. We are shown the aftermath, and sometimes—as with Parkland—we see victims hiding or escaping. But we don't see what the bullets actually do."[48]

—Jamelle Bouie, a reporter for the online magazine *Slate*

survivors of school shootings. But a vigorous debate about how to prevent future gun massacres in schools requires that the public be given all the facts—even if those facts are hard to stomach.

Blaming the Media to Shift Responsibility

Assigning blame to media coverage for school shootings is often just an attempt to shift responsibility from someone else's failures. The media are an easy target. News outlets do compete for the most sensational details about a story like the Parkland shootings. And trust in the media has fallen in recent years. But concern about the media should not distract the public from those who actually do bear some responsibility for school shootings.

For example, gun rights groups often come under fire after a school massacre. They know that a disturbed young shooter's access to guns is a legitimate issue that puts them on the defensive. After Parkland, gun control once more became a hot topic, with students there organizing the Never Again movement. Feeling the heat, pro-gun spokespeople tried to divert blame to the media. A few days after the Parkland shootings, gun rights activist Colion Noir declared:

> No one on this planet benefits more from mass shootings and motivates more people to become mass shooters than our mainstream media. Sure, they love to get up in front of the camera and sell the lie that the mass shootings are all the NRA's [National Rifle Association's] fault, and falsely claim that the NRA is a soulless organization selling guns to killers for profit. But all my years of watching these events play out have led me to one conclusion: The mainstream media love mass shootings.[49]

Such outrageous statements are an obvious attempt to change the subject in the glare of the national spotlight.

But gun rights activists are not the only ones who try to escape accountability after a school shooting. Sometimes school officials or law enforcement will tell media outlets to back off when they fear their own failures could be exposed. Months after the Parkland shootings, the Broward County School Board and state attorney's office refused to release the security camera footage taken during the massacre. Authorities claimed that releasing the footage could jeopardize students at MSD High School by revealing details about the security system. However, many suspected the real reason was to protect those who failed to do their jobs. Several Broward County deputies seem to have taken cover during the six-minute shooting spree instead of rushing the building. "The footage is the only objective evidence of what occurred and when," says Barbara Petersen, president of the First Amendment Foundation, which joined media outlets in suing for the footage. "Access to the video footage allows us to hold those accountable who may not have done their jobs."[50]

The media should continue to cover school shootings to satisfy the public's right to know about these violent incidents. With responsible coverage, media outlets can help spark important debates about how to prevent gun violence in schools. And news organizations must not be diverted from their mission by those who seek to shift blame and cover up their own failings. The news media is far from perfect, but it is a vital part of our democratic system.

Source Notes

Overview: School Shootings and Violence

1. Quoted in Venita Fritz, "Marshall Superintendent Says Mental Health the Key Issue in Preventing School Shootings," *Kentucky New Era* (Hopkinsville, KY), July 12, 2018. www.kentuckynewera.com.
2. Quoted in Mandy Mayfield, "Trump After Florida Shooting: No One 'Should Ever Feel Unsafe in an American School,'" *Washington Examiner*, February 14, 2018. www.washingtonexaminer.com.
3. Quoted in Elizabeth Chuck et al., "17 Killed in Mass Shooting at High School in Parkland, Florida," NBC News, February 14, 2018. www.nbcnews.com.
4. Quoted in Martin Kaste, "Despite Heightened Fear of School Shootings, It's Not a Growing Epidemic," NPR, March 15, 2018. www.npr.org.
5. Quoted in Mike Stunson, "After Mass Shooting, Kentucky School District Bans Backpacks at Most Schools," *Lexington (KY) Herald-Leader*, June 6, 2018. www.kentucky.com.

Chapter One: Should Schools Be Equipped with Metal Detectors?

6. Rebecca Wendlandt, "Metal Detectors Save Lives," *Spokane (WA) Spokesman-Review*, March 4, 2018. www.spokesman.com.
7. Quoted in Anna M. Tinsley and Diane Smith, "Metal Detectors: Can They Prevent Mass Shootings at Schools?," *Fort Worth (TX) Star-Telegram*, February 28, 2018. www.star-telegram.com.
8. Quoted in Zach Winn, "The Pros and Cons of Installing Metal Detectors in Schools," *Campus Safety*, April 27, 2018. www.campussafetymagazine.com.
9. Quoted in Corey Williams, "With Security Measures, Urban Schools Avoid Mass Shootings," *Chicago Sun-Times*, March 19, 2018. www.chicago.suntimes.com.
10. Quoted in AOL, "Metal Detectors Installed at All Schools in New Jersey District," March 29, 2018. www.aol.com.
11. Quoted in Tinsley and Smith, "Metal Detectors."
12. Ken Trump, "School Metal Detectors," National School Safety and Security Services. www.schoolsecurity.org.

13. Paul Powers, "School Metal Detectors Would Cost $98 Million a Year in S.C., but Some Say They're Worth It," *Charleston (SC) Post and Courier*, February 12, 2018. www.postandcourier.com.

14. Quoted in Lia Fernandez, "Gun Slips Through Middle School Metal Detector," WRDW.com, January 10, 2019. www.wrdw.com.

15. Quoted in Madina Toure, "Use of Metal Detectors in New York City Schools Under Scrutiny amid Parkland Shooting," *Observer*, March 9, 2018. www.observer.com.

16. Quoted in Danny Katch, "NYC Students Get Metal Detectors Expelled," SocialistWorker.org, January 19, 2018. www.socialistworker.org.

Chapter Two: Should Teachers and Staff Members Be Armed?

17. Starr Sackstein, "Teachers Should Not Have Guns," *Work in Progress* (blog), *Education Week*, February 27, 2018. www.blogs.edweek.org.

18. Quoted in Cindy Long and Tim Walker, "Arming Teachers Is Not the Answer," NEA Today, March 5, 2018. http://neatoday.org.

19. Quoted in Long and Walker, "Arming Teachers Is Not the Answer."

20. Quoted in Maureen Downey, "Union to Trump: Teachers Don't Want to Be Armed; We Want to Teach," *Atlanta Journal-Constitution*, February 28, 2018. www.ajc.com.

21. Joshua Grubbs, "Why I Won't Bring My Gun into My Classroom," CityLab, February 23, 2018. www.citylab.com.

22. Quoted in Louis Freedberg, "Push to Arm Teachers in California Would Face Major Hurdles," EdSource, February 23, 2018. https://edsource.org.

23. Daniel Payne, "Of Course We Should Let Teachers Carry Guns in School," *Washington Examiner*, February 20, 2018. www.washingtonexaminer.com.

24. Whitney Blake, "There's Simply No Sense in Allowing Schools to Remain Soft Targets for Killers," Federalist, March 7, 2018. www.thefederalist.com.

25. Quoted in Erica L. Green and Manny Fernandez, "Trump Wants to Arm Teachers. These Schools Already Do," *New York Times*, March 1, 2018. www.nytimes.com.

26. Quoted in Nicole Chavez, "These Schools Say Arming Teachers 'Can Be Done Right,'" CNN, February 28, 2018. www.cnn.com.

Chapter Three: Should Schools Have Mental Health Counseling Programs?

27. Noam Shpancer, "Improved Mental Health Care Won't Prevent Mass Shootings," *Psychology Today*, March 27, 2018. www.psychologytoday.com.

28. Barbara Bradley Hagerty, "The Futility of Trying to Prevent More School Shootings in America," *Atlantic*, May 21, 2018. www.theatlantic.com.

29. Quoted in ABC7 Chicago, "Dimitrios Pagourtzis: What We Know About the Santa Fe Shooting Suspect," May 18, 2018. www.abc7chicago.com.

30. Jonathan Foiles, "Mental Illness Didn't Make Him Do It," *The Thing with Feathers* (blog), *Psychology Today*, February 15, 2018. www.psychology today.com.

31. Shpancer, "Improved Mental Health Care Won't Prevent Mass Shootings."

32. Quoted in Julio Ochoa, "Parents Are Leery of Schools Requiring 'Mental Health' Disclosures by Students," NPR, September 21, 2018. www.npr .org.

33. Nancy Barile, "The Importance of Mental Health Awareness in Schools," Hey Teach! www.wgu.edu.

34. Quoted in Kate Santich, "Central Florida Schools Get Millions of Dollars for Mental-Health Services After Parkland Shooting," *Orlando Sentinel*, August 11, 2018. www.orlandosentinel.com.

35. Quoted in Tim Walker, "Are Schools Ready to Tackle the Mental Health Crisis?," NEA Today, September 13, 2018. http://neatoday.org.

36. Katie Hurley, "We Need to Provide Better Mental Health Treatment in Schools. Here's How to Start," *Washington Post*, January 6, 2017. www. washingtonpost.com.

37. Quoted in Kevin Mahnken, "The Hidden Mental Health Crisis in America's Schools: Millions of Kids Not Receiving Services They Need," 74, November 7, 2017. www.the74million.org.

38. Quoted in Mahnken, "The Hidden Mental Health Crisis in America's Schools."

Chapter Four: Does Media Coverage Contribute to the School Shootings Problem?

39. Quoted in Mike James, "Parkland's Nikolas Cruz Made Chilling Videos Before Shooting: 'You're All Going to Die,'" *USA Today*, May 30, 2018. www.usatoday.com.

40. Quoted in James, "Parkland's Nikolas Cruz Made Chilling Videos Before Shooting."

41. Quoted in Adam Harris, "The Media's Week-Long Attention Span for a Mass Shooting," *Atlantic*, November 15, 2018. www.theatlantic.com.

42. Quoted in Maggie Fox, "Mass Killings Inspire Copycats, Study Finds," NBC News, July 2, 2015. www.nbcnews.com.

43. Quoted in Lois Beckett, "Texas High School Shooting Prompts Talk of 'Contagion Effect,'" *Guardian* (Manchester), May 19, 2018. www.the guardian.com.

44. William Cummings, "Why Active Shooter Training Didn't Help in the Florida High School Shooting," *USA Today*, February 16, 2018. www.usatoday.com.

45. Jared Keller, "Does the Media Cause Mass Shootings?," *Pacific Standard*, October 3, 2016. www.psmag.com.

46. Quoted in Aaron Feis, "'You're All Going to Die': Chilling Videos Show Nikolas Cruz Plotting Attack," *New York Post*, May 30, 2018. www.nypost.com.

47. Quoted in Jamelle Bouie, "Show the Carnage," *Slate*, February 15, 2018. https://slate.com.

48. Bouie, "Show the Carnage."

49. Quoted in German Lopez, "The NRA Just Released an Absurd, Offensive Video Blaming the Media for Mass Shootings," Vox, February 22, 2018. www.vox.com.

50. Quoted in Nicholas Nehamas, "What Did Deputies Do During Parkland Shooting? Officials Fight to Keep Footage Secret," *Miami Herald*, July 11, 2018. www.miamiherald.com.

School Shootings and Violence Facts

Expanding School Security

- Since the Columbine shootings in 1999, school security has become a multibillion-dollar industry. Security companies market sophisticated surveillance equipment to schools. They also provide high-priced consultants to manage the technology.
- According to the National Center for Education Statistics, 19 percent of public schools had security cameras during the 1999–2000 school year. By the 2015–2016 school year, that number had grown to 81 percent.
- According to a market analysis by IHS Markit, revenue for school security equipment and services totaled $2.7 billion in 2017.
- Some public schools are installing facial recognition technology. Under this system, only people whose faces are stored in data banks can enter the school building. In 2018 the tech firm RealNetworks began offering facial recognition technology for free to K–12 schools in Seattle, Washington.

Anxiety About School Shootings

- A March 2018 study from the Pew Research Center found that 57 percent of US teens ages thirteen to seventeen admit that they are at least somewhat worried that a shooting could happen at their school. According to the study, 25 percent of US teens are very worried about the possibility of a shooting attack at school.
- The Pew Research Center study also found that 73 percent of Hispanic students and 60 percent of black students were at least somewhat worried that a shooting could occur at their school. This compares to only 51 percent of white students.

- According to the 2017 national Youth Risk Behavior Survey conducted by the Centers for Disease Control and Prevention, 6.7 percent of students reported that they missed class in the previous month because of worries about their safety at school.
- A 2018 PDK International poll on attitudes toward education found that 34 percent of parents say they fear for their child's safety at school. This percentage is nearly three times more than that in 2013.

Common Factors in School Shootings

- According to Nadine Connell, an associate professor of criminology and director of the Center for Crime and Justice Studies at the University of Texas–Dallas, shooters almost always attack their own schools. Connell notes that attacks on schools are rarely carried out by strangers.
- School shooters are overwhelmingly male. Of the thirty-two school shootings since 1990 in which three or more people were killed, only one of the perpetrators was female.
- The vast majority of school shootings occur in suburban areas or small towns. Only five of the thirty-two major school shootings since 1990 took place in large cities.
- Most school shooters get their guns from home or a family member. School shooters tend to be obsessed with guns, violent video games, and violent movies.
- According to psychologist George S. Everly of the Johns Hopkins University School of Medicine, school shooters exhibit an obsessive quality that leads them to plan an attack in great detail. They also seem unable to understand the consequences of their actions, which may account for their frequent run-ins with police or school authorities.

School Shootings and Gun Control

- After the school shooting in Parkland, Florida, thirty-two states passed or considered adopting so-called red flag laws, which allow law enforcement to seize firearms from individuals judged to be a threat. Six states already had such laws before Parkland.

- In June 2018 student survivors of the Parkland school shooting made a sixty-day, twenty-state bus tour to promote gun control. The tour was part of the Never Again movement, aimed at ending school shootings with tougher gun control laws.
- Opinion polls by Gallup, Quinnipiac, and others showed that support for stricter gun control laws reached a twenty-year high following the school shootings at MSD High School and Santa Fe High School.
- Compared to the general population, students ages thirteen to seventeen are slightly less in favor of raising the minimum age for purchasing a firearm.

Related Organizations and Websites

Brady Campaign to Prevent Gun Violence
840 First St. NE, Suite 400
Washington, DC 20002
website: www.bradycampaign.org

The Brady Campaign to Prevent Gun Violence and its many local chapters seek to create a safer America by ending America's epidemic of gun violence. It works for responsible gun ownership and strict enforcement of gun laws in existence to stop gun violence, including school shootings.

Brookings Institution
1775 Massachusetts Ave. NW
Washington, DC 20036
website: www.brookings.edu

The Brookings Institution is a progressive think tank based in Washington, DC. It studies and makes policy recommendations about today's most important issues, including school shootings and violence. The Brookings Institution website includes features about school shootings, including "To Make Schools Safer, Focus on Community—Not Guns."

Center for American Progress (CAP)
1333 H St. NW
Washington, DC 20005
website: www.americanprogress.org

CAP is an independent policy institute dedicated to improving the lives of all Americans through bold, progressive ideas, strong leadership, and concerted action. The CAP website contains articles and podcasts on school shootings and gun control.

The Heritage Foundation

214 Massachusetts Ave. NE
Washington, DC 20002
website: www.heritage.org

The Heritage Foundation's mission is to formulate and promote conservative public policies based on the principles of free enterprise, limited government, individual freedom, and traditional American values. Its website includes recent articles such as "Parkland-Style Shootings Are Devastating but Highly Unusual" and "3 Common Traits of School Shooters."

National Association of School Psychologists (NASP)

4340 East West Highway, Suite 402
Bethesda, MD 20814
website: www.nasponline.org

The NASP is a professional group representing more than twenty-five thousand school psychologists, graduate students, and related professionals worldwide. The NASP works to advance effective practices that improve students' learning, behavior, and mental health. The NASP website features many articles about school shootings, school safety, and how to prevent violence in schools.

National Education Association (NEA)

1201 Sixteenth St. NW
Washington, DC 20036
website: www.nea.org

The NEA is the nation's largest professional employee organization, with affiliate groups in more than fourteen thousand communities across the nation. The NEA is committed to advancing the cause of public education. Its website includes many articles and features about school shootings and how teachers can deal with student anxieties about school violence.

National Rifle Association (NRA)
11250 Waples Mill Rd.
Fairfax, VA 22030
website: www.NRA.org

The NRA is America's foremost defender of Second Amendment rights as well as the world's premier firearms education group. The NRA believes stricter gun-control laws are not the answer to school shootings and lobbies to maintain gun rights in state legislatures.

Never Again MSD
@NeverAgainMSD

Never Again MSD is an American student-led political action committee that promotes gun control. It was formed by a group of students at Marjory Stoneman Douglas High School in the wake of the shootings there in February 2018. Never Again MSD has organized several events, including the March for Our Lives, a nationwide demonstration demanding action on gun violence.

Sandy Hook Promise
13 Church Hill Rd.
Newtown, CT 06470
website: www.sandyhookpromise.org

Sandy Hook Promise is an organization that seeks to prevent gun-related deaths due to crime, suicide, and accidental discharge of a gun. The group, formed after the school shooting at Sandy Hook Elementary School in Newtown, Connecticut, emphasizes how to recognize signs of tendencies toward violent behavior and how to prevent gun violence from erupting in schools.

For Further Research

Books

Sue Klebold, *A Mother's Reckoning: Living in the Aftermath of Tragedy.* New York: Broadway, 2017.

Peter Langman, *School Shooters: Understanding High School, College, and Adult Perpetrators.* Lanham, MD: Rowman & Littlefield, 2017.

Sarah Lerner, *Parkland Speaks: Survivors from Marjory Stoneman Douglas Share Their Stories.* New York: Crown Books for Young Readers, 2019.

Jaclyn Schildkraut and H. Jaymi Elsass, *Mass Shootings: Media, Myths, and Realities.* Santa Barbara, CA: ABC-CLIO, 2016.

Bradley Steffens, *Gun Violence.* San Diego: ReferencePoint, 2020.

Bradley Steffens, *Gun Violence and Mass Shootings.* San Diego: ReferencePoint, 2019.

US Secret Service, *2018 Secret Service School Shooting Reports.* Washington, DC: US Department of Homeland Security, 2018.

Internet Sources

Jonathan Foiles, "Mental Illness Didn't Make Him Do It," *The Thing with Feathers* (blog), *Psychology Today*, February 15, 2018. www.psychologytoday.com.

Andrew Griffin, "Should Teachers Carry Guns in Classrooms? The Arguments After Donald Trump Suggests Schools Without Guns Are 'Magnets' for Massacres," *Independent* (London), February 22, 2018. www.independent.co.uk.

Adam Harris, "The Media's Week-Long Attention Span for a Mass Shooting," *Atlantic*, November 15, 2018. www.theatlantic.com.

Lauren Porosoff and Jonathan Weinstein, "Opinion: To Prevent School Shootings, Can Mental Health Be Taught?," *PBS NewsHour*, March 6, 2018. www.pbs.org.

Jaclyn Schildkraut, "The Media Should Stop Making School Shooters Famous," Vox, March 31, 2018. www.vox.com.

Anna M. Tinsley and Diane Smith, "Metal Detectors: Can They Prevent Mass Shootings at Schools?," *Fort Worth (TX) Star-Telegram*, February 28, 2018. www.star-telegram.com.

Index

About the Author

John Allen is a writer who lives in Oklahoma City.